FERRIES

OF THE ISLE *of* MAN

1945 ~ present day

STAN BASNETT

Published on the Isle of Man by
 Lily Publications, PO Box 33, Ramsey, Isle of Man IM99 4LP
Tel: +44 (0)1624 898446 Fax: +44 (0)1624 898449
E-mail: info@lilypublications.co.uk Web: www.lilypublications.co.uk

INTRODUCTION

Ferries of the Isle of Man is the seventh book in the Transport Features series. Once again it is a personal collection of photographs, this time of passenger ships that have sailed to and from the Isle of Man over the last fifty years. It includes a number of cargo vessels which had limited passenger facilities and which are relevant to the developing story, particularly as the shipping scene entered the era of all-year-round ro-pax services.

Those who may have read the first book in the series will have learnt that my grandfather had a great influence on my interest in really anything that happened in and around Douglas harbour from a very young age. He was well known to many of those involved with the Steam Packet Company and I was taught how to recognise ships from a distance by their individual characteristics. This was something which my mother perpetuated and so I was encouraged (or was it indoctrinated?) to observe all that was going on all around me!

One of my most vivid memories of this time was being present on the King Edward Pier when the *Lady of Mann* arrived still in her battleship grey after the war before being de-commissioned. The reason being that my grandfather, being a shareholder and proud of the war service of the steamer, wanted to be there to see her arrive back safely. He also knew the Chief Engineer and we went on board and I was shown around the engine room - a little boy's dream. I suppose it was that single event that fired my interest in shipping and left a lasting impression and fondness for that particular ship. Strangely even now I have a vivid memory of walking along the passageway to the engineers' cabin and seeing signs above the doors in blue glass with the names illuminated by natural light, 'Gentlemen's Hairdressing', in the dark bowels of a ship, being the one that I couldn't understand for years.

The Liverpool & North Wales Steamship Co. Ltd. vessel *St. Seiriol* (2) unusually berthed alongside the King Edward Pier Viaduct and discharging passengers on a day trip from Llandudno. Compare this location with the present harbour layout! *(Author's collection)*

I have been asked why did we choose Transport Features as the title for the series. I was encouraged in my early forays into photography by Bill Peters and Derek Taylor of Manx Press Pictures and in my teens together with Bill and John Gaggs, a long-term school pal and senior sixer in the 9th Douglas Cubs who became a press photographer, to produce a series of copy transparencies under the collective title of Transport Features. The venture is long since defunct and so when the opportunity arose to revise an earlier publication of Ferries of the Isle of Man I had very little difficulty in persuading the publisher Miles Cowsill to adopt the title. Little did I realise just how much time putting the series together would take. Fortunately two other local enthusiasts have taken on two of the series which has eased the load considerably.

For those of you who are unfamiliar with the Isle of Man, it is situated in the middle of the Irish Sea. Although part of the British Isles it is not part of the United Kingdom and is in fact a Crown Dependency with its own governmental system. Traditionally it was more or less four hours' sailing from either Ireland or England and about five hours from Eire or Scotland. Now with the introduction of fast craft on these routes the times have been significantly reduced.

The island lies on its long axis roughly north and south with the Point of Ayre at its northern extremity and the Calf of Man at its southern. The main port and capital of the island is Douglas situated on the east coast, now with modern terminal facilities, two ro-ro berths and a cargo marshalling area. Prior to the extension of the breakwater at Douglas vessels would be diverted to Peel on the west coast in the event of Douglas being subjected to easterly gales. Ramsey in the north of the island was an occasional port of call for vessels on passage to Ardrossan and Belfast until 1970

The *King Orry* (3) and *Mona's Queen* (3) at the Victoria Pier in the late 1930s showing the lines and size of the company's flagship to advantage. She was the ultimate in cross-channel development at the time. *(Author's collection photo by the late Paul Barton)*

This photograph of the IOMSPCo steamer **Lady of Mann** (I) has been seen before but I make no excuse for including it as it is my favourite photograph of the vessel, seen leaving Douglas in September 1965.

when a fall in demand and the deteriorating condition of the Victorian iron pier led to the closure of the berthing head.

Naturally being an island makes it almost entirely dependent on sea transport for most of its essential supplies. Passenger and goods traffic between the island and the UK evolved through Liverpool but through circumstance has now centred on Heysham although fast craft services still operate to Liverpool and other ports in the British Isles. For passenger travel between the adjacent islands there is the alternative of a comprehensive system of air routes as well as the all-year-round sea route to Heysham.

The island has a long maritime tradition and its development as a holiday destination has its roots in the Victorian predilection of "taking the waters"; the tourist industry, so long the life-blood of the island, was built up around it. This led to the formation of the Isle of Man Steam Packet Co. and other shipping companies that plied the Irish Sea trade. The Steam Packet, as it is still affectionately known, was formed in 1830 and it is still going strong, which makes it one of the oldest shipping companies in the world.

The island's growth owes much to the tourist industry, which was for many years its mainstay. The prosperity continued for almost two decades after the Second World War after which the effect of cheap holidays abroad started to make its impact on the island and indeed many other traditional UK seaside holiday destinations. The immediate post-war expansion of the Steam Packet fleet bore witness to this wealth.

At one time in the post-war period there were as many as eight passenger vessels in service in the summer months. The first car ferry, **Manx Maid**, was introduced in 1962, prior to which cars were carried on the conventional passenger ships and craned on and off. The car ferry was unusual in so

This photograph was taken shortly before the **Ben my Chree** (4) left Douglas for the last time at midnight on 12th September 1965 after thirty-eight years' service with the company.

The **Ben my Chree** arriving at the King Edward Pier on a summer evening in 1960. A Ramsey Steamship coaster, the **Ben Ain**, is at the breakwater and the rowing boats are secure at Circus Beach, finished for the day - idyllic!

far as she was designed as a side-loading vessel using internal ramps to cope with the large tidal ranges at ports around the Irish Sea. This may have seemed like a retrograde step in view of the development of ro-ro services taking place elsewhere. However, this must be tempered with the lack of facilities that existed at Douglas and most of the other ports served by the company. There was also the problem of the island's financial situation at that time and a general downturn in its economy, which meant that there was insufficient funding available for major port improvement, although the new Sea Terminal at Douglas was just nearing completion.

The design of the side-loader must have been successful as it paved the way for three other vessels, two of which were the first diesel-engined passenger ships owned by the company.

The 1970s saw a revolution in the type of vessel serving the island; a rival ferry company in the

form of Manx Line appeared on the scene and introduced the first ro-ro service to the island using Heysham as its UK terminal and providing its own linkspan at Douglas. The subsequent development of that company and the involvement of Sealink saw a great variety of ferries on service to the island. Fast craft appeared at the same time and were set to change sea travel to the island for ever, eventually forming the backbone of the Liverpool and Irish services. The competition for the finite business led inevitably to a merger of the two companies under the Steam Packet banner.

The island was now starting to enjoy new-found wealth in the finance sector which the Manx Government had encouraged to replace the emphasis on the seasonal tourism which by this time was a shadow of what it had been. This in its turn led to funding becoming available for the breakwater extension at Douglas and the associated much-needed harbour improvements

including a second linkspan, which remains Government owned. The island was playing catch up.

The first edition of this book covered thirty years of ferries serving the island and much has happened in the last decade to warrant this revised and updated second edition. The photographs now cover the last fifty years and show how the post-war ferry scene around the island has changed. It mirrors in many ways what has happened throughout the whole of the British Isles but because the island is only thirty miles in length and eleven wide with a population now in the region of eighty thousand it is easier to digest in an island context.

With the bulk of freight and passenger traffic now handled by one conventional ro-pax vessel and one fast craft year-round there have been a surprising number of different vessels chartered to cover seasonal peaks of both freight and passenger flows as well as surveys. The opportunity has been taken in this edition to rearrange the photographs in some sort of chronological order although it is not intended to be a comprehensive record. I have included some vessels not strictly ferries that have served the island where there is a tale to tell. Again it is a personal choice from my own photographs and includes, as before, some from Miles Cowsill who is now an island resident. Here they are, then, and I hope that you find them interesting.

Over the years I have counted among my friends many Masters and officials of the various companies and also Harbour Masters and other officials, all of whom have been extremely tolerant to my camera often recording events which at the time they wished I hadn't! This collection is a tribute and a big "thank you" to them.

I hope it whets your appetite to come and visit the island, which is a gem in the Irish Sea holding many more treasures within its shores.

Stan Basnett
Glen Vine

This photograph of the *Victoria* laid up at the Tongue is not very good quality but I include it because it is the first photograph I took of any Steam Packet vessel. The camera was an old Kodak Brownie box camera and the picture was taken whilst I was still at school, as far as I can remember in 1952 or 1953.

Still with the **Ben-my-Chree** (4) (above), this time leaving Douglas in a southerly gale with the wind holding the vessel against the Victoria Pier as the Master slides her down the Pier unable to lift her off as she takes the morning Liverpool departure. By contrast here is the "**Ben**" with an evening arrival (below) approaching the North side of the Victoria Pier.

I was anxious to take as many photographs of the "old Ben" before she went and so nearly all of the ones included were taken in 1965. The "Ben" is berthed at the Victoria Pier (top) but the interest is really in the **Manxman** (2) berthed at the Battery Pier on what was referred to as the lay-by berth. The "**Ben**" is seen arriving Douglas (bottom), once again straight in for the Victoria Pier with an evening arrival from Liverpool in June 1965.

Now we are with the **Lady of Mann** which was the consort to the **Ben-my-Chree**. This is the engineer's control stand with the engine telegraphs positioned ahead of the control valves. All a far cry from today's direct control from the bridge and reversible pitch propellers.

Both the "**Lady**" and the "**Ben**" retained the charm of a past way of travel and nowhere was this more apparent than in the dining rooms - yes, two dining rooms - they were originally two-class vessels. This is the Second Class dining room and it still had table cloths and silver service.

The **Lady of Mann** calling at Ramsey Queens Pier which was a scheduled port of call for Belfast and Ardrossan services even in the 1960s. Unusually She is berthing at the "Liverpool berth" on the south side of the Pier. Perhaps the wind which is from the north has too much east in it as this berth was more often used with the wind from an easterly direction.

The "**Lady**" heading for the south side of the King Edward Pier and showing her classic lines and counter stern as she glides past the head of the Battery Pier. The engineer no doubt just bleeding on some astern steam anticipating the telegraph. There was not a lot of room on this berth which was the favoured winter berth before the extension of the breakwater.

Here is the **King Orry** (4) at that very berth having stopped before hitting the bar across the harbour, after which the rest of the harbour was tidal, but the river has got the wrong side of the bow and is holding it off the pier. A bit of judicious work with the engines should get the stern close and the heaving line strategically hanging from the fo'c'sle can be got ashore and the capstan would do the rest.

Not an easterly gale but nonetheless a strong easterly breeze which has sent all the vessels out into the bay to anchor to avoid ranging against the pier, while the **King Orry** approaches the Victoria Pier to discharge her passengers before joining the rest in the bay until required to load.

The *King Orry* coming alongside the Queens Pier at Ramsey on a Belfast trip during 1968. Even then the Pier would move alarmingly if the vessel came down hard on the berthing head.

It is without doubt August judging by the mist hanging about and the fact that all the vessels of the IOMSPCo. are on service. You could guarantee fog during the first two weeks of August but it was not normal to encounter a stiff south easterly breeze at the same time. Here the **Tynwald** (5) dating from 1947 is leaving in just those conditions.

The *Tynwald* leaving Ramsey for Douglas having called at Ramsey Queens Pier on passage from Ardrossan. These Sunday calls were superb. You could travel by tram to Ramsey from Douglas, ride along the Queens Pier tramway and get the boat back to Douglas. What a way to spend an afternoon!

The IOMSPCo. vessel **Snaefell** (5) was built in 1948 and served the company for twenty nine years before being scrapped. She was the fifth of six post-war sister ships all built for the company by Cammell Laird & Co. Ltd. Two photographs from the 1960s of the ship arriving at Douglas. The Sea Terminal has been completed this was one of the significant changes to the harbour at that time but it really came too late and was never used as originally designed.

Now two photographs of the **Mona's Isle** (5) which was the fifth of the post-war sister ships. She entered service three years after the **Snaefell** and also lasted twenty-nine years before being broken up in Holland in 1980. Believe it or not both photographs were taken in the summer on different occasions as she left Douglas.

September 1965 and the same day as the photograph in the Introduction. The **Lady of Mann** leaves the Victoria Pier with many competitors and officials from the 1965 International Six Days Trial on board leaving the island after the event.

Here is the **Mona's Isle** coming alongside Peel breakwater having been diverted from Douglas due to easterly gales on 17th February 1966. She was sharing the winter sailings with the **Manxman**.

The **Mona's Isle** surfing in to Douglas with a following sea left over from a southerly gale which always created a troughing swell across the harbour approach. The deepening of the approach following the breakwater extension diminished this effect considerably.

The summer of 1967 and the **Mona's Isle** in this photograph is berthed at the King Edward Pier bow, out having been warped around the head of the pier earlier in the day due to an excessive swell in the outer harbour causing her to range against the **Snaefell** where she had been double-berthed overnight.

Well I did say that I was going to be a bit liberal in my interpretation of ferries and so I am with these two photographs. The *Fenella* (3) was the first motor ship owned by the IOMSPCo. and an unusual but I think very striking cargo ship. She could carry up to twelve passengers but as far as I know this facility was really only used by persons accompanying horses or cattle.

This was the last steam single hatch coaster to operate on the Irish Sea routes and the photograph shows the *Conister* (1) being towed away by the tug *Campaigner* on 26th January 1965 for breaking up. It was to signify the end of an era.

The **Manxman** (2) seen here approaching the King Edward Pier on winter service was the last of the post-war sister ships, all of which had some slight differences. The most noticeable in the case of the **Manxman** was the manner in which the lifeboats were carried. She also had the latest type of Pametrada patent steam turbine engines.

It really was unusual to see one of the Steam Packet boats, I don't think we ever called them ferries, leave Douglas bow first until the advent of the bow thrusters on the car ferries - now we always refer to them as ferries. I have no idea why the **Manxman** left in this manner on 19th April 1965 as the weather was calm but once again the vessel was warped around the head of the pier before getting under way with the 4 pm Liverpool sailing.

The photographs which Frank Hodson and I took on the morning of Tuesday 16th November 1965 became quite well known. These are two of a number I managed to take. The top one has been seen before but the bottom one hasn't been published before. The Liverpool sailing to the island that day was cancelled. The **Manxman** took eight hours to cross to Liverpool but had no alternative other than to leave due to the exposed nature of Douglas at that time to easterly gales.

This 1959 photograph of the **King Orry** approaching Liverpool landing stage (above) shows her still with the cravat on top of the funnel. It was removed two years later as it had suffered from severe corrosion and the company considered on the advice of the Engineering Superintendent that they need not replace it. The result (below) is that she ran for another fourteen years without it!

The **Mona's Isle** approaching the north side of the King Edward Pier. Note the semaphore on the Harbour Master's office indicating which berth to use. The year is 1961, the spire of the Sea Terminal is nearing completion and only requires post-stressing. The **King Orry** is the other vessel in the picture.

1962 saw the arrival of the first car ferry built for the Steam Packet to meet a very particular specification. The Steam Packet came in for criticism for not building a ro-ro vessel which was by that time coming on scene. As the company pointed out Douglas and a number of other ports they served did not have ro-ro facilities. This arrival at Peel being a case in point, the **Manx Maid** (2) (above) having been diverted because of easterly gales. The normal port of arrival was Douglas but even overnight the fickle weather of the Irish Sea surrounding the island could spring some surprises. Instead of moderating the weather could increase and catch a vessel in port exposed to an easterly gale, leaving her no alternative other than to sail as we have seen with the **Manxman** in 1965. Here the car ferry **Manx Maid** (below) is photographed leaving into the teeth of an easterly gale in September 1967.

A photograph from September 1959 of the **King Orry** arriving at the Liverpool landing stage, and the distinctive cravat on the funnel is clearly seen.

Ancient and modern - another example of the old order changing which of course is a reflection of life. Here the **Lady of Mann**, the grand old lady, was the flagship of the company but in her last few years, making a difficult approach to Victoria Pier No.1 berth and passing the latest addition to the fleet **Manx Maid** occupying No.2 berth. Why difficult? Well, there was not a lot of room and with the tide low and not a lot of water the "**Lady**" had to get her nose in at all costs before hitting the ferry steps or grounding on Circus Beach.

The car ferries were popular for Round the Island trips with the car ramps being open to the public and entertainment provided by the Onchan Silver Band, another good way to while away a Sunday, particularly on a sunny day passing Laxey going north about. The old Steam Packet deck chairs are still in evidence, having been retained when the earlier vessels were scrapped.

1971 was to be the **Lady of Mann**'s last season with the company so I thought it appropriate to include another photograph of her at Ramsey Queens Pier in July 1968.

(Above) In 1969 Norwest Hovercraft formed a company to operate the Fleetwood-Isle of Man service in opposition to established services by the Steam Packet Co. They chartered the Norwegian vessel **Stella Marina** although she was a ro-ro vessel She never operated as such simply because of the lack of port facilities. What it did do, however, was open the eyes of islanders to the comforts of modern sea travel. It was a wake-up call for the Steam Packet but was ignored.

(Right) The paddle steamer **Waverley**, berthed at the King Edward Pier, was a summer visitor as part of the round Britain excursions run by the vessel.

The **Mona's Isle** approaches the King Edward Pier and as I mentioned earlier the post-war sister ships although similar had some external differences which I insisted should be learnt by my daughters, sub-consciously perpetuating what my grandfather had done with me. You can amuse yourself within these pages counting the differences in the number of lounge windows on the front of these ships and the side cutaways in the promenade and shelter decks.

No prizes for identifying the **Manxman**!

Norwest Hovercraft which had set up in opposition to the Steam Packet Co. in 1969 with their chartered vessel **Stella Marina** with so much promise chartered the **Queen of the Isles** during the middle of May 1970 while their newly acquired vessel **Lochiel** was being prepared for service. She is seen arriving at Douglas.

In 1970 Norwest Hovercraft purchased the **Lochiel** which had belonged to David MacBrayne to maintain their newly established service. She proved to be a disaster. The ship entered service on Saturday 6th June 1970. It proved to be under-powered, suffered numerous engine failures and had difficulty maintaining sailing schedules. Marooned and irate passengers often had to be flown back to Blackpool at the company's expense. The final straw came when the vessel grounded on a sandbank on 27th July off Fleetwood and the passengers had to be taken off by Fleetwood lifeboat! Continuing engine trouble forced the company to cease trading with the last sailing taking place on 13th August and they did not operate the following year.

This is the last photograph I am going to include of the 'Lady' in her last year of operation making a spectacular arrival at No.2 berth, Victoria Pier. She has to carry some way to negotiate the narrow approach to this berth on a flood tide but then stop in a hurry to avoid hitting the *Tynwald* berthed just ahead of her. It all looks very close from the wheelhouse and not for the faint-hearted.

Some more photographs which are hardly ferries but which I hope you enjoy nonetheless. Here the **Balmoral** is leaving Douglas on one of its evening departures from Douglas to Whitehaven during one of its seasonal passages around Britain.

The **St Trillo** formerly of the Liverpool & North Wales Steamship Co., Ltd. was in Manx waters during May 1967 acting as tender to the visiting cruise liner **Kungsholm**.

The *Stena Sailer* was on charter to the Steam Packet during May 1983 while the *NF Jaguar* was undergoing major overhaul before coming to the Steam Packet on demise charter.

The *Balmoral* arriving at Peel after a somewhat choppy crossing from Belfast in September 1989 during another season of coastal cruises.

The island suffered severely from the effects of the National Union of Seamen's Strike which started on Sunday 15th May 1966. It was to last until midnight on Friday 1st July. The strike dealt a disastrous blow to the holiday trade. The TT races were cancelled and the Steam Packet men were hit as hard as anyone, but with the strike over, Saturday 2nd July saw a crowd of 2000 welcome the *Manxman* back to Douglas with the Town Band in attendance and drum majorettes! There were at least a hundred people on the end of the breakwater. I don't think anyone realised in that moment of euphoria that irreparable damage had been done to the Steam Packet.

Without any shadow of doubt this was the coldest I have ever been anywhere in the world taking a photograph! The *Snaefell* arriving at Peel in a full easterly gale and a snowstorm in January 1970.

By 1966 the car ferry **Manx Maid** was already in service and performing extremely well for the Steam Packet. It wasn't surprising that the company ordered a running mate. The **Ben-my-Chree** (5) sailed on her maiden voyage on 12th May three days before the Seamen's Strike. She couldn't have had a worse baptism. Nonetheless the two car ferries successfully ran the winter service until the arrival of the first motor passenger car ferries sailing in all weathers.

The 'Ben' suffered in the early days with problems with her boiler burners and I always thought that the engineers must have had a grudge against the navigating officers who had to face this onslaught on the bridge wing!

The **Ben-my-Chree**
departing, on a not really
typical winter day, into the
tail of a southerly gale
when the residual fetch on
the sea would send big
unbroken swells across the
harbour entrance which
would certainly test the
seaworthiness of any vessel.
These two ferries were
fitted with stabilisers but
they could not be deployed
before leaving and would be
largely ineffective until the
vessel was under way.

Just to prove a point that car ferries did call at Ramsey I have included these two photographs of the **Ben-my-Chree** coming alongside the berthing head on the Queens Pier in 1968 and leaving onward for Ardrossan.

Not to be outdone here is a photograph of the **Manx Maid** arriving at Douglas across the same swell I have mentioned earlier. Now, since the breakwater extension and more significantly since the Conister Flakes have been blasted away for the new approach channel, it is possible to approach almost head into the offending swell.

Here the **Ben-my-Chree** has missed the approach to Peel breakwater and is stuck across the sand bar formed by the River Neb running past the breakwater on its discharge to sea. Further difficulty is caused when the stern swings out and the easterly wind gets the wrong side of it. It calls for some hefty work on the heaving lines!

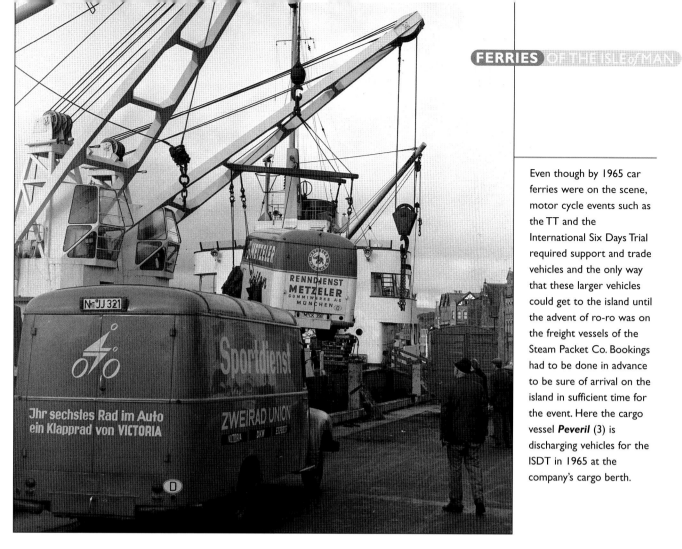

Even though by 1965 car ferries were on the scene, motor cycle events such as the TT and the International Six Days Trial required support and trade vehicles and the only way that these larger vehicles could get to the island until the advent of ro-ro was on the freight vessels of the Steam Packet Co. Bookings had to be done in advance to be sure of arrival on the island in sufficient time for the event. Here the cargo vessel *Peveril* (3) is discharging vehicles for the ISDT in 1965 at the company's cargo berth.

Double-deck buses would be carried to the island across the foredeck of either the *King Orry* or the *Manxman*. Both had sections of removable rail to allow the buses to be driven off at Douglas. This photograph is of the *Manxman* arriving on 12th December 1968 with an AEC Regent MkV double-deck bus for the Douglas Corporation.

In this photograph the car ferry **Ben-my-Chree** (5) is turning in the "croak" or outer harbour at Douglas using the steam driven bow thruster which was retro fitted after the Masters of the company had experienced the value of bow thrusters fitted to the **Mona's Queen** which was the first of the diesel-engined car ferries.

A calm afternoon as the **Tynwald** arrives at Ramsey Queens Pier. It is worth remembering that, before the car ferries, accompanied private cars and motor cycles were carried on the shelter deck of these passenger ships. Depending on the length of the vehicles there would be between 20 and 22 cars carried, with a reduction in the passenger certificate when cars were carried. Cars were usually driven on at Liverpool landing stage but craned off at Douglas.

The *Manxman* under way and showing to good effect the cruiser stern and hull form that the Steam Packet adopted after the success of the *Fenella* and *Tynwald* of 1936

In 1972 the IOMSPCo. took delivery of their first motor passenger ship the **Mona's Queen** (5). Fitted with controllable pitch propellers, stabilisers and a bow thruster unit she proved to be a very manoeuvrable vessel and revolutionised berthing. Now we would see vessels turning in the outer harbour and leaving bow first as a matter of routine. This eventually led to the bow rudders being welded solid.

An unusual scene with the **Mona's Queen** alongside the Alfred Pier at Port St. Mary in 1990 when the vessel visited the port to meet the local Commissioners and other dignitaries as part of a promotional drive to increase awareness of the company and as a "thank you" for the island's patronage.

The last time that horses
came for the horse
tramway in Douglas direct
from Northern Ireland was
in January 1971 when the
Slieve Donard arrived in
the middle of the night on
passage to Liverpool to
unload the horses which on
this occasion were not
walked to the stables.

45

During her first two-and-a-half years the **Mona's Queen** ran on the winter service with one of the earlier car ferries. It was usually the **Ben-my-Chree** as it was the custom to put the newest vessels on the winter run and get them revenue earning. It is a nice winter shot as she crosses that swell.

Another view of the **Mona's Queen** at Port St. Mary.

The company were so well pleased with the new motor ship that a second followed in June 1976. She was launched in December 1975 from the Ailsa Shipbuilding yard at Troon, and became the second vessel to carry the name *Lady of Mann*. She entered service in June the following year and is seen arriving at Douglas in the evening of the day she entered service.

The *Lady of Mann* (2) in pristine condition and on service in 1976 approaching Douglas. The Steam Packet Co. now had four side-loaders in service and still hadn't responded to the threat coming from IOM Ferry Express which was taking most of the freight from the company and was soon to introduce a ro-ro service to the island.

The **Manxman**, the last conventional passenger ferry to be operated by the IOMSPCo., arriving at Peel under the command of Capt. Tom Corteen having been diverted from Douglas due to easterly gales.

The latest vessel to be operated by the Steam Packet is the ro-pax vessel **Ben-my-Chree** (6) introduced in 1998. She is the sixth ship to carry the name which in Manx Gaelic literally means "girl of my heart" or colloquially "sweetheart". She is photographed arriving at Douglas with the afternoon sailing from Heysham and shows the alterations made to form an additional lounge just aft of the lifeboat.

Guilty I'm afraid. It is another photograph of the "old Lady", this time approaching the Ramsey Queens Pier from the north and calling on passage to Douglas with a good complement on board.

Something that would never happen now and last happened in the 1960s. The **King Orry** is berthed, in June 1965, on the cattle steps at the Battery Pier.

The **Viking III** arriving at Douglas while on charter to Manx Line during October 1980.

Another late afternoon photograph of the *Tynwald* leaving Ramsey Queens Pier heading for Douglas.

TYNWALD

DOUGLAS

TWIN SCREWS
KEEP CLEAR
OF
PROPELLERS

The **Mona's Isle** approaches the breakwater at Peel.on 17th February 1966. Hardly a hint that it is winter except for a scattering of snow on the top of Greeba in the far distance.

You have seen the double-deck bus arriving on the **Manxman** already but I didn't mention that they were loaded by crane at Liverpool. They were, however, driven off at Douglas onto the King Edward Pier and they had four minutes to do it on either a rising or falling tide.

The **Manx Viking** in her original Manx Line colours leaving Douglas, in October 1979, into an easterly swell, showing just how exposed Douglas was to even the slightest weather from the east.

An interesting photograph of the **Manx Maid** leaving Douglas into a full south-easterly gale in September 1967. The vessel has her screws out of the water, no doubt giving the engineers some cause for concern. In these conditions the Captain would have to take the ship well out into the bay before securing the bow rudder and turning. The short wave pattern of the Irish Sea meant that these vessels were either supported amidships or at either end by the wave crest giving that familiar, but uncomfortable, feeling as the ship sank into the following trough. A feeling now replicated by the fast craft in similar conditions. The photograph overleaf of the **Ben-my-Chree** further illustrates this point.

A photograph of the Sealink/SNCF vessel **Villandry** leaving Douglas with an evening sailing for Heysham in June 1983. The vessel was on charter to Manx Line during the latter part of June and into July 1983.

The *Ben-my-Chree* arriving at Douglas in a south-easterly gale and a following sea. The size limitations of Douglas harbour meant that the length of these ships was limited to about two-and-a-half average wave lengths in the Irish Sea which is why they were so lively compared with longer vessels on the Irish routes. This is clearly illustrated in this photograph and the earlier one of the *Manx Maid* leaving in similar conditions.

During November 1979 the Sealink vessel *Dalriada* was chartered by Manx Line to cover for the *Manx Viking* which was undergoing repair at Barrow. Here again is that easterly slop which is catching the stern just as the vessel leaves Douglas harbour

Here is the **Snaefell** of the IOMSPCo. at last alongside the breakwater at Peel after the second attempt at entering the port on that dreadful day in January 1970. (see page 36)

The *Lady of Mann* arriving at Peel on 4th December 1977 late in the afternoon after a stormy passage from Liverpool.

You could almost guarantee gales around the equinoxes but the island situated as it is slap-bang in the centre of the Irish Sea could expect bad weather any time and in 1977 it experienced a fairly difficult winter, although not as bad as the winter of 1964/65.

The photograph shows the *Lady of Mann* heading out of Douglas into the tail of a southerly gale which always swept the island with these big swells.

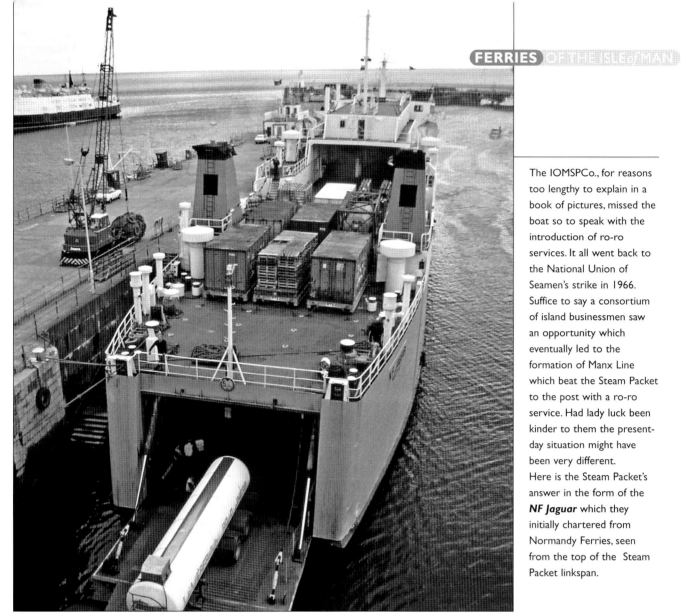

The IOMSPCo., for reasons too lengthy to explain in a book of pictures, missed the boat so to speak with the introduction of ro-ro services. It all went back to the National Union of Seamen's strike in 1966. Suffice to say a consortium of island businessmen saw an opportunity which eventually led to the formation of Manx Line which beat the Steam Packet to the post with a ro-ro service. Had lady luck been kinder to them the present-day situation might have been very different.

Here is the Steam Packet's answer in the form of the **NF Jaguar** which they initially chartered from Normandy Ferries, seen from the top of the Steam Packet linkspan.

The **Stena Sailer** was chartered by the Steam Packet during May 1983 when the **NF Jaguar** was undergoing dockyard work prior to purchase by the company.

In June 1988 the Isle of Man Government chartered the **Bolette** from Fred Olsen Lines anticipating trouble arising from a dispute with the National Union of Seamen which in the event didn't materialise. The vessel did perform some runs to relieve peak traffic problems and also ran a Round the Island trip.

The saga of the Steam Packet Co.'s sixth **Mona's Isle** was one of woe and best forgotten. It was a shame really because the vessel, the former Townsend **Free Enterprise III**, held such promise. Although nineteen years old at the time of purchase she was still potentially a suitable vessel for the Steam Packet routes and an attractive vessel to boot - or at least in my eyes.

Due to problems associated with alterations carried out for the company she only remained in service less than a year - being sold in October 1985.

The *Lady of Mann* secure alongside the breakwater at Peel at ten past four on Saturday 3rd. December 1977 having had a rough crossing in a south-easterly gale. The entry to Peel was a bit spectacular, passing the head of the pier at about 10 knots with the propellers full astern and the bow thrust holding her off the pier. The inevitable heavy clout against the pier knocked most of the speed off and discharge was complete within five minutes! Too much excitement!

The **Lady of Mann** arriving at Douglas after completion of a £2.6 million renovation which was carried out prior to the start of the 1989 season. The main purpose was to increase her car-carrying capacity but with a reduction in her passenger certificate. The alterations internally were reflected in a quite different outward appearance. *(Miles Cowsill)*

The **Riverdance** was chartered by the Steam Packet in May 2002 at very short notice to cover for the **Ben-my-Chree** which had to enter dry dock for emergency repairs. The vessel handled the freight traffic while passengers were conveyed on the fast craft.

Two more charter vessels for the IOMSPCo. The P&O ro-ro vessel **Lion** (above) enters Douglas on charter, while the **Ben my Chree** was off service for bi-annual survey purely to handle the freight traffic. An accident with the **Lady of Mann** had the knock-on effect of causing a backlog of freight vehicles at Heysham at the height of the summer season. It was cleared by the **Saga Moon** (below), in June 1993, on short-term charter by the company expressly for that purpose.

I have already mentioned Manx Line which has been creeping into the story and so now is the time to look at it in more detail. Manx Line grew out of Ronagency/IOM Ferry Express which in turn grew out of the NUS strike of 1966. The first indication that Manx Line was serious was when the ro-pax vessel *Monte Castillo* (above) arrived at Douglas for berthing trials on 23rd December 1977 before going to Glasgow for alterations to satisfy the Board of Trade for transfer to the British Register. The next step was the arrival of a purpose-made linkspan (below), provided by Manx Line, on 27th June 1978.

Manx Line suffered a series of setbacks which would have seen many throw in the towel but persevere they did and for the full story you should read MANX LINE by Ferry Publications as it takes a whole book to relate! Late at night on 1st December 1978 the linkspan broke adrift in an easterly gale, putting the new service out of action.

The newly acquired vessel now named *Manx Viking* was diverted to Peel, arriving at 8 pm where the passengers were disembarked, but of course being a stern-loader the cars couldn't be off-loaded.

Reminiscent of Norwest Hovercraft before, the **Manx Viking** was beset with mechanical problems. Requiring charter vessels to cover the service, the company being anxious not to lose any of its hard-won freight contracts. Sealink's **Dalriada** was chartered to cover while the **Manx Viking** was under repair.

The **Viking III** was chartered to provide cover for the **Manx Viking** away on survey during the period between 28th February and 30th March 1980. She was a very popular ship with the travelling public and was back again for a short period in September; on 5th October she ran a well supported Round the Island cruise despite a south-westerly gale!

The **Viking III** leaving Douglas in mid October 1980 with the **Manx Viking** still not back in service. By this time Sealink had become involved with Manx Line, offering effectively a rescue package for the company, and things would improve dramatically. By this time the Steam Packet were clearly becoming worried about the effect on their freight trade.

This photograph of the Steam Packet's **Ben-my-Chree** at the King Edward Pier before their linkspan was in place and **Viking III** at the Manx Line linkspan in its second stage of development in 1980 illustrates just how far the Steam Packet were behind the game, having ignored the warning signs of the success of their fledgling competitor.

The *Manx Viking* had been for annual survey early in 1980 but later dropped a valve in one of her engines which saw the vessel out of service for a short time with the *Lagan Bridge* being one of two vessels brought in to clear the freight backlog, the other being the *Lune Bridge*.

The breakwater extension at Douglas was not completed until 1983 and even though some work had been done to protect the linkspan easterly gales saw the *Manx Viking* diverted to Peel again.

By the end of 1980 with discussions well advanced with Sealink, Manx Line could now draw on their resources for vessels to cover for the **Manx Viking**, the **Ailsa Princess** (left) and **Antrim Princess** (below) both seeing winter service between Heysham and the Isle of Man.

Now the Steam Packet were really worried because they were losing serious amounts of freight traffic.

The **Antrim Princess** was to cover for the **Manx Viking** between October 1980 and January 1981 while Sealink engineers tried to get to the bottom of the problems with **Manx Viking**.

The **Antrim Princess** was diverted to Peel on 2nd November 1980 due to conditions at Douglas and discharged passengers only who were taken to Douglas by bus. It was to be three days before their cars were discharged at Douglas! The vessel would eventually come into Steam Packet ownership as the **Tynwald** (6).

Another photograph of the **Ailsa Princess** leaving Douglas in March 1983 covering for the **Manx Viking** which was once again away for annual survey. The company by this time was known as Sealink Manx Line and the Heysham service was being marketed throughout the Sealink empire with a consequent further upturn in business. Inevitably rumours started about a possible merger of the two companies serving the island.

The **Antrim Princess** making a spectacular entry to Douglas during her time on service with Sealink Manx Line in late 1980.

The IOM Steam Packet Co. and Caledonian MacBrayne operated a summer-only service between Scotland and the island during 1994 and 1995 which was not successful and abandoned the following year. Here is the *Claymore*, which was the vessel employed on the service, arriving at Douglas in the first summer of operation.

Familiar? Well, it should be - the former *Antrim Princess* now in Steam Packet colours is photographed on Victoria Pier No.1 berth. The vessel was time-chartered by the Steam Packet from October 1985 for almost five years following the debacle with the *Mona's Isle*. She was renamed *Tynwald* in 1986.

The *Lune Bridge* (left) seen leaving Douglas and turning in the harbour approach, was the other vessel chartered by Sealink Manx Line during TT week in 1980 to clear the backlog of freight caused by the failure of the *Manx Viking*. The Steam Packet embarked on a cross-channel ro-ro venture operated by a subsidiary company, which was not successful, using the *Belard* (below), a former P&O vessel. She covered for the *Peveril* on occasion and is seen at the King Edward Pier, on what became known as the Government linkspan, before the installation of the overhead passenger walkway.

Two photographs of the *Earl Godwin*, another Sealink vessel which covered for the **Manx Viking** during her 1981 annual survey. Arriving at Douglas on 25th March 1981 (above) and approaching the linkspan (right) unusually berthing bow in to discharge over the bow.

The **Earl Godwin** again in
the outer harbour at
Douglas showing the
graceful lines of these
vessels to good advantage.

The Sealink/SNCF vessel *Villandry* under the French flag was collected at short notice from Dover by a crew from Sealink Manx Line to cover for **Manx Viking** at the height of the season from 23rd June to 10th July 1983. The photographs show the vessel turning in the outer harbour and leaving Douglas with the bow visor still not fully secured. This practice was to stop following the tragic loss of the **Herald of Free Enterprise** in 1987.

Two photographs here of the **Manx Viking**, in Sealink colours (above) and sporting the three-legged emblem fitted to the funnels in Holyhead during her 1981 annual survey as she turns in the outer harbour to go astern onto the Victoria Pier linkspan. The photograph (below) shows her leaving Douglas in Steam Packet colours after the merger of the two companies in 1985.

Another of those small Townsend Thoresen vessels the **Viking Victory** showing her attractive lines as she approaches the linkspan on 9th April 1981. If Manx Line had been able to use one of these vessels at the outset the whole story of the company might have been totally different.

In 1981 the Steam Packet had at last seen the threat and the **Peveril** (3) was to leave the island in June, by which time they would have installed their own linkspan and chartered a ro-ro freight vessel. In this photograph the **Peveril** is at the Steam Packet cargo berth which had remained in use by them during the time they had tried to compete with ro-ro with their container lift-on lift-off service.

The *European Mariner* was on charter to the Steam Packet from 21st January to 11th February 2002 covering for the new *Ben-my-Chree* which was away for refit.

The Centenary of the TT races gave the Steam Packet major problems which saw their new flagship devoting her space to motorcycles and accompanying trade vans. Several freight ro-ro vessels were chartered to handle the additional freight generated by an almost doubling of the population for a fortnight. Here is the *Hoburgen* of Norfolkline leaving Douglas on 28th May 2007.

I have jumped ahead a bit too far because the Steam Packet acquired one of their best ships in recent years after the **Tynwald** and before the **Ben-my-Chree**. In 1990 and already eighteen years old the former train ferry **Saint Eloi/Channel Entente** entered service with the company being re-named **King Orry** (5) later in the year and retaining its white livery. *(Miles Cowsill)*

Eventually the **King Orry** carried traditional Steam Packet livery and really it was not as imposing as the white livery. Both photographs on this page show the "Liverpool door" which was fitted after her acquisition to allow side loading at Liverpool landing stage. Proving once again the wisdom of the side-loading philosophy. *(Miles Cowsill)*

The **Peveril** formerly **NF Jaguar**, in full Steam Packet colours turns in the outer harbour before going astern onto the old Steam Packet linkspan on the south side of the King Edward Pier. This second-hand acquisition by the Steam Packet proved to be a good investment and offered limited accompanying driver accommodation. She stayed in service with the company for sixteen years. She is seen here arriving on her final sailing in 1998 from Heysham. *(Miles Cowsill)*

The **Lady of Mann** arriving at Douglas during TT races, operating in tandem with the **Ben-my-Chree**. *(Miles Cowsill)*

In 1998 the Steam Packet accepted delivery of their newest and largest ship. The **Ben-my-Chree** was built by Van der Giessen-deNoord in Rotterdam. She is photographed leaving Douglas and is in her original condition without the additional lounge accommodation fitted later.*(Miles Cowsill)*

The new breakwater at Douglas may well provide protection for vessels within the harbour but you can see from this photograph that as soon as a vessel pokes its head out into a south-easterly it knows about it!
The **Ben-my-Chree** is photographed butting into that swell I keep writing about.

A Captain's eye view looking aft from the wheelhouse of the ***Ben-my-Chree***.

Fast craft were introduced to the island in 1994 and **Seacat Isle of Man**, a 74m wave-piercing-craft, was the precursor of many. She is photographed, in one of the many liveries she has carried, arriving off Douglas and lifting on one of those shelving swells.

This is the 81m WPC **Seacat Rapide** arriving at Douglas and in the process of undergoing one of the many name changes that the fast craft seem to have as an in-built part of their DNA!

The Steam Packet have employed a number of different fast craft on their services and here is the *Seacat Scotland*. Some have even appeared more than once carrying different names. This view of her on Victoria Pier No.2 berth shows the beam of these craft and the twin hulls which house the engines - two in each hull. She was berthed at the Victoria Pier during December 2000 while Fort Street Engineering (the engineering arm of the Steam Packet Co.) carried out essential maintenance.

The *Superseacat Three* registered in La Spezia was built in 1999 by Fincantieri in Italy for Sea Containers Ferries Scotland. In 2000 she was chartered to the IOM Steam Packet Co. and is photographed on the King Edward Pier linkspan from the marshalling area on the Circus Beach infill.

The **Superseacat Two** (above) now in Steam Packet livery at Victoria Pier No.1 berth and the **Superseacat Three** (below) turning to drop onto the Victoria Pier linkspan. Both photographs show the sleek lines of these MDV1200 class fast craft. The sleek lines are hardly surprising as the design concept comes from the Pininfarina organisation and anyone my age immediately associates that name with fast cars in particular Ferrari. The cat nomenclature adopted by Sea Containers is a misnomer because the craft are not as you can see catamarans but are single-hull vessels with a hard chine hull and behave like an overgrown powerboat. I have to admit I like them!

Here on charter to the Steam Packet for TT traffic is the P&O *Express* turning in the outer harbour. This is the largest of the Incat wave piercing craft which have been on service to the island to date at 91m. The Steam Packet Company have now in 2008 been successful in acquiring an even larger 96m Incat WPC, due to enter service in 2009 with a service speed of 35 knots and having a higher wave height capability. This should ensure less interruption to winter schedules for fast craft sailings.

The P&O *Express* provided Irish services to the island mostly during the night in her normal stand-down time but here she is photographed on 31st May 2007 leaving Douglas on one of her rare daylight visits during the Centenary TT festival.

I know that these two ships are not ferries but I did promise myself that latitude in the Introduction. The island plays host to numerous visiting cruise ships and I include these because of their special relationship. The expedition cruise ship *Explorer* (above) being assisted by Laxey Towing Co.'s. **Wendy Ann** berthing in windy conditions was a regular visitor on some of her British Isles cruises. She collided with unseen ice floes in the Antarctic in November 2007 and sank and passengers had to abandon ship. They were rescued fortunately very quickly by the **Nordnorge** which was also on an Antarctic cruise - she had also visited the island and was photographed alongside the north side of the Victoria Pier in 2001.

The **Dart I** at the King Edward Pier linkspan, chartered by the Steam Packet to handle freight traffic while the **Ben-my-Chree** was away early in 2000 for her first survey. She was the first of these large standard freighters which were to become a familiar mid-season sight at Douglas.

The **River Lune** was chartered from Norse Merchant Shipping for freight duty during TT week 2005, the **Ben-my-Chree** being devoted to passenger traffic and bikes and associated vehicles arriving for the TT. The **River Lune** had previously been owned by Cenargo until 2003 when the company went into liquidation,

The **Seacat Diamant** was chartered from Sea Containers for the 2005 TT period, mostly running on the Heysham route. The **Diamant** was originally employed on the Dover-Calais route by Hoverspeed Ltd. and these larger 81m WPC Seacats are ideally suited for the Irish Sea. She was not available long term to the Steam Packet and so it was something of a missed opportunity.

In the 1960s the Steam Packet would be running eight vessels during the TT festival with some weekends seeing almost continuous ship movements in and out of Douglas. 2007 was very reminiscent of those days. Here is the Norfolkline freight vessel **Hoburgen** turning in the outer harbour.

The Seatruck *Riverdance* (above), later to come to grief off Blackpool, was another of the vessels
chartered to handle the anticipated extra freight traffic arriving at the Island for the 2007 TT. Here she is
seen from Head Road turning in the outer harbour prior to dropping down onto the King Edward Pier
linkspan to discharge. Cobelfret's *Phocine* (below) also on charter for that period sits on the same berth
waiting to load.

The *Saga Moon* was yet another freight vessel chartered by the Steam Packet to handle freight backlogs and cover for the *Ben-my-Chree*, She is photographed leaving Douglas.

The *Stena Caledonia* was chartered for two weekends over the 2007 Centenary TT celebrations and again in 2008. She is photographed at the King Edward Pier linkspan on 2nd June 2007.

The **CFF Seine** ex **Dart 3** was also chartered for the same reasons. The name changes of these vessels reflect the highly volatile nature of shipping businesses in the present day.

The **Ben-my-Chree** was due for survey in March 2008 but this was delayed until April due to the unavailability of suitable charter craft to handle the freight traffic. Eventually the Steam Packet were able to secure Seatruck's **Triumph** on sub-charter for the period. A superb modern freight ro-ro vessel indicative of the larger vessels employed on Irish Sea routes. Any bigger and they will not be able to use Douglas!

TT week 2008 saw the Steam Packet chartering additional freight capacity once again. Here the **East Express** having taken the Douglas Harbour Pilot on board continues her approach to Douglas on 9th June 2008 she was photographed from the pilot boat.

The **Sea Express1** emerged early in May 2008 in her latest guise in modern Steam Packet-style colours and renamed **Snaefell** (6) following its major repair after sustaining serious damage in a collision in the Mersey in February 2007.

Two photographs showing the remaining two fast craft being operated by the Steam Packet in the latest colours reflecting the old company livery, looking very smart and both carrying new names for the 2008 season. The *Snaefell*, formerly *Sea Express 1*, ex *Seacat Isle of Man* (above) passes HMS *Ark Royal* in Douglas Bay on 9th June 2008 while the *Viking* (2) formerly *Superseacat Two* (below), leaves Douglas sporting her new very smart livery and clearing residual fuel from a cold start-up.

Not all of the vessels which the IOMSPCo. have owned have gone to the breakers and it would not be possible within the confines of this book to cover them all. However, here is a "where are they now" page covering two of the more recent vessels which have gone on to a life after the Steam Packet. The **King Orry** was photographed (above) by Bruce Peter under Moby Line ownership as the **Moby Love**. The **Lady of Mann** is barely recognisable after her major alterations to enable a limited number of freight vehicles to be carried in addition to cars. Renamed **Panagia Soumela** she is shown (below) heading away from Limnos at dawn during July 2007 in this photograph by Richard Seville.

Caledonian Princess arriving at Douglas with a Stranraer Town Band charter on 20th June 1968. This was the first time that one of the new generation of ro-ro car ferries had called at Douglas and her arrival was spectacular, particularly her speed through the harbour entrance, the advantage of bridge control being immediately apparent.

Manx Viking photographed in the Lune Deep on passage to the Isle of Man in June 1982, the vessel in full Sealink livery after her Holyhead re-fit in March 1981 during which the three legs emblem was fitted to the funnels. The ship was now operating at her best with the full resources of Sealink behind her – what a different story it would have been had this been the situation four years earlier!

FERRIES
OF THE ISLE of MAN

1945 ~ present day

STAN BASNETT

Transport Features of the Isle of Man is the collective title for a series of books presenting a photographic record of various modes of transport to, from and in the Isle of Man as recorded by a number of writers living in the island and seen from an island perspective.

The seventh book in the series is a revision and update of Ferries of the Isle of Man Past and Present and includes a number of photographs not previously published. It was the revision of this earlier booklet that led to the publication of the Transport Features series.

In addition to presenting a pictorial record of the island's passenger shipping over more than half a century, it also records significant changes which have taken place around the ports of the Isle of Man which in many ways reflect the changes nationally.

The author of the book although best known for his photographs of shipping has recorded many aspects of island life particularly with regard to transport over the last 50 years.

Trains of the Isle of Man – The twilight years

Trains of the Isle of Man – The Ailsa years

Trains of the Isle of Man – Post nationalisation

Buses of the Isle of Man – 1945 – present day

Planes of the Isle of Man – 1945 – present day

Trams of the Isle of Man – 1946 – present day

Ferries of the Isle of Man – 1945 – present day

Coastal Shipping of the Isle of Man – 1946 – present day

Published on the Isle of Man by

 Lily Publications, PO Box 33, Ramsey, Isle of Man IM99 4LP

Tel: +44 (0)1624 898446   Fax: +44 (0)1624 898449

E-mail: info@lilypublications.co.uk   Web: www.lilypublications.co.uk

ISBN 978-1-906608-03-3

9 781906 608033

£15.00

Double-Deck Trams of the World

Beyond the British Isles

Brian Patton

Alexandria. A scene at Sporting Club on 6 June 1961 with rebuilt double-decker 502 and single-deck motor car 501. (Raymond de Groote)

Alexandria. Balcony car 58 on left and rebuilt car 525 on right at Place Zaghoul on 6 June 1961. (Raymond de Groote)

Durban's official last tram, 7015, on the last run, Tuesday 2 August 1949. (Kevan J. Marden collection)

Barcelona. Class B double-decker 197 at Plaza Palacio on 14 June 1957. (Raymond de Groote)

A monsoon day in the Fort district of Bombay in 1961 with car 2, one of the post-war trams, and a tower wagon. (Hugh Ballment)

Bombay. Car 154, one of those built during the war, at Flora Fountain in 1961. (Hugh Ballment)

Johannesburg, 1945. Booysens (Turffonte Route) where road crosses SAR 'mineral' line and mine ropeway crosses road. (B.T. Cooke)

Preserved Hobart 46 on a low loader in Elizabeth Street on its first outing in 1993. (Ian Cooper)